WEATHER and CLIMATE

Earth's Climate

Robin Birch

Marshall Cavendish
Benchmark

New York

This edition first published in 2010 in the United States of America
by Marshall Cavendish Benchmark.

Marshall Cavendish Benchmark
99 White Plains Road
Tarrytown, NY 10591
www.marshallcavendish.us

All Internet sites were available and accurate when sent to press.

First published in 2009 by
MACMILLAN EDUCATION AUSTRALIA PTY LTD
15–19 Claremont Street, South Yarra 3141

Visit our website at www.macmillan.com.au or go directly to www.macmillanlibrary.com.au

Associated companies and representatives throughout the world.

Library of Congress Cataloging-in-Publication Data

Birch, Robin.
    Earth's climate / by Robin Birch.
        p. cm. – (Weather and climate)
    Summary: "Discusses the climate zones on Earth"–Provided by publisher.
    Includes bibliographical references and index.
    ISBN 978-0-7614-4471-8
    1. Climatic zones–Juvenile literature. 2. Earth–Juvenile literature. I. Title.
    QC981.8.Z6B57 2009
551.6–dc22

                                                    2009004980

Edited by Kylie Cockle
Text and cover design by Marta White
Page layout by Marta White
Photo research by Legend Images
Illustrations by Gaston Vanzet

Printed in the United States

Acknowledgments
The author and the publisher are grateful to the following for permission to reproduce copyright material:
Front cover photograph: CloudSat satellite courtesy of NASA
Photos courtesy of:
© 5ugarless/Dreamstime.com, 7; © Icefields/Dreamstime.com, 12; © Ivonnewierink/Dreamstime.com, 6; © Kamchatka/
Dreamstime.com, 5; © Tondafoto/Dreamstime.com, 13 (top); © sebastien burel/iStockphoto, 11; © David Freund/iStockphoto,
29; © Jan Gottwald/iStockphoto, 19; © Richard Gunion/iStockphoto, 22; © Joe Hodgson/iStockphoto, 25; © Ah Huat Tan/
iStockphoto, 9 (bottom); © Tobias Johansson/iStockphoto, 17; © Ljupco/iStockphoto, 4; © Howard Oates/iStockphoto, 26;
© ranplett/iStockphoto, 9 (top); © mark rigby/iStockphoto, 15; © Kitch Bain/Shutterstock, 13 (bottom); © Pichugin Dmitry/
Shutterstock, 10; © FloridaStock/Shutterstock, 23; © Inger Anne Hulbækdal/Shutterstock, 20; © John Kirinic/Shutterstock, 21;
© Chee-Onn Leong/Shutterstock, 30; © Vinicius Tupinamba/Shutterstock, 24.

While every care has been taken to trace and acknowledge copyright, the publisher tenders their apologies for any accidental
infringement where copyright has proved untraceable. Where the attempt has been unsuccessful, the publisher welcomes
information that would redress the situation.

1 3 5 6 4 2

Contents

Glossary Words

When a word is printed in **bold**, you can look up its meaning in the Glossary on page 31.

Weather and Climate

What is the weather like today? Is it hot, cold, wet, dry, windy, or calm? Is it icy or snowy? Is there a storm on the way? We are all interested in the weather because it makes a difference in how we feel, what we wear, and what we can do.

The weather takes place in the air, and we notice it because air is all around us.

Weather Report

Hikers need to know if the weather is safe for walking in the wilderness. Sailors and fishers also need to be informed about the weather, so they know if it is safe to be on the water.

These people are experiencing good weather conditions for mountain trekking in Macedonia.

Earth's Climate

The word *climate* describes the usual weather of a particular place. If a place usually has cold weather, then we say that place has a cold climate. If a place usually has hot weather, we say it has a hot climate. There are many different climates around the world.

When we talk about Earth's climate, we mean the usual weather of the whole world. It is also a way to talk about all of Earth's different climates at the same time. For example, we may say that Earth's climate is changing. This would mean that some or all of the climates around the world are changing.

The Sahara Desert has a hot climate.

Weather Report

The study of climate is called climatology. Scientists who study climates are known as climatologists.

Climate Zones

This island is in a tropical climate zone.

Around the world there are many different climates. We say that places with similar climates are in the same climate zone. There are nine climate zones, which means there are nine different climates on Earth. Each of the nine climate zones can be found in more than one country. The arid climate zone, for example, can be found in African countries, the United States, Australia, and other countries.

The nine climate zones are:

- tropical
- subtropical
- arid
- semiarid
- Mediterranean
- temperate
- northern temperate
- polar
- mountain

Word	Meaning
tropical	the area around the **equator**
sub	less than
arid	dry
semi	not as extreme
Mediterranean	as found around the Mediterranean Sea
temperate	moderate or mild
northern	to the north
polar	around the North and South **Poles**
mountain	on mountains

Climate Zones Map

A climate zones map shows the different climate zones of the world. Each climate zone is shaded a different color.

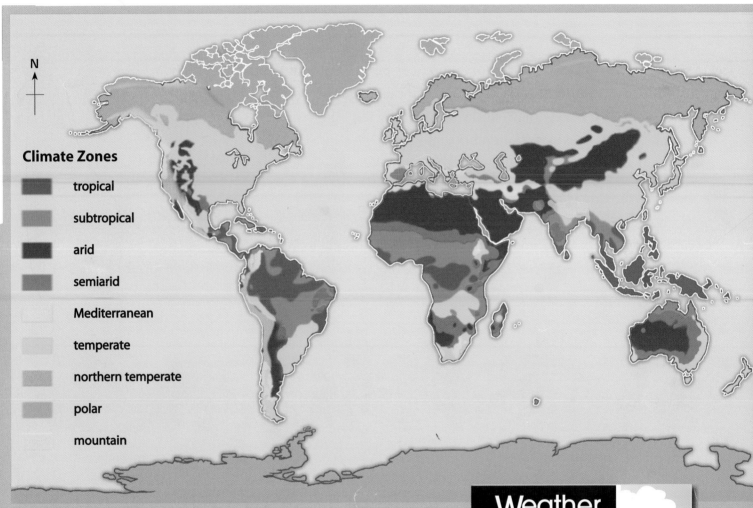

Climate Zones

- tropical
- subtropical
- arid
- semiarid
- Mediterranean
- temperate
- northern temperate
- polar
- mountain

There are nine different climate zones on Earth.

Weather Report

The driest climate zone is the arid zone. Deserts are found here. The coldest climate zone is the polar zone, found around Earth's North and South Poles.

Finland is in a polar climate zone, so it is very cold.

Tropical Zone

In the tropical zone, the weather is hot and **humid**. The sky is often cloudy and there is lots of rain. Lush **forests** grow, and plants have brightly colored flowers and fruits.

Places with a tropical climate are found near Earth's equator. These places all have high **temperatures**, humidity, and rainfall for all or most of the year. Because the air is very moist and is warmed by the Sun, **cumulus** clouds develop most afternoons, often bringing rain.

Temperatures are high in the tropical zone because the Sun is always overhead or almost overhead in these areas. The heat and light from the Sun do not change very much during the year.

Weather Report

In the tropical zone, the temperature difference between day and night is usually only a few degrees.

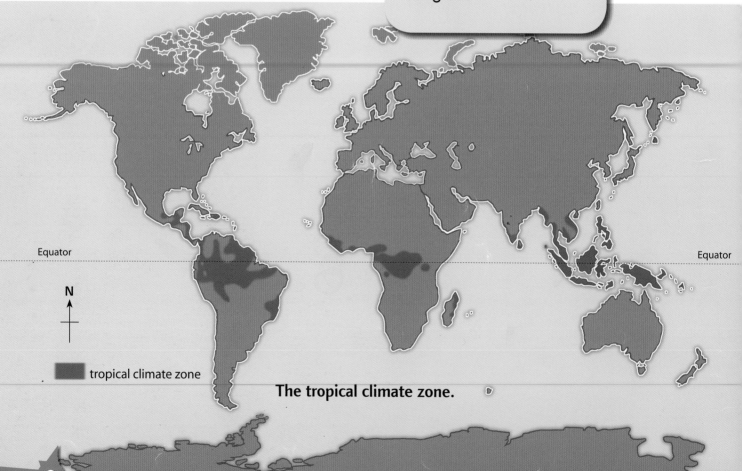

Equator

N

tropical climate zone

The tropical climate zone.

Vegetation

In the tropical zone, we mainly find tropical **rain forests** growing. This is because there is a lot of light, warmth, humidity, and rain all year. Trees and other plants grow quickly in this climate.

In rain forests, the upper branches of the trees grow so close together that they make a roof for the forest, called a canopy. The canopy blocks out light, so lower down in the forest it is darker and plants do not grow thickly. Around the edges of rain forests, where there is a lot of light, there is very thick **vegetation**. This vegetation is commonly called jungle.

Plants in rain forests have leaves with drip tips and waxy surfaces so water runs off, which keeps the leaves healthy. Some plants climb or grow on top of others to reach sunlight. Flowers are brightly colored to attract insects.

Animals

Animals in the tropical zone are suited to living in warm, wet conditions. The basilisk, for example, is a lizard that can run across the surface of water.

The keel-billed toucan is native to the tropical rain forests of Belize in Central America.

Selangor, Malaysia, has a steamy, humid environment.

Subtropical Zone

The subtropical zone has a climate similar to a tropical climate, except it has both rainy and dry seasons. This climate is found in a wide band north and south of tropical climates. It can be near the equator or some distance from the equator.

In the subtropical zone the climate is warm all year. The rainy season is very humid. During the dry season, these areas can get hotter than the tropical zone because hot winds from hot **deserts** blow over them.

Weather Report

Some subtropical areas have monsoon winds, which blow out to sea in the dry season and bring heavy rain when they blow from sea to land in the wet season.

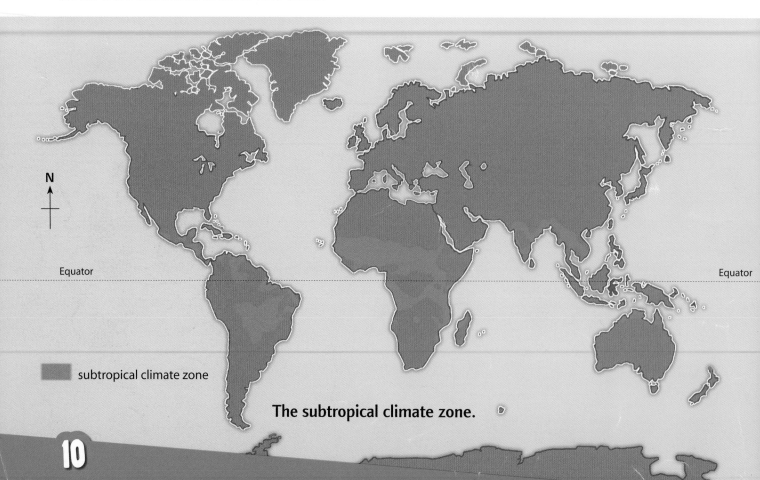

Equator   Equator

subtropical climate zone

The subtropical climate zone.

Vegetation

Grasslands and open **woodlands** are found in the subtropical zone. Woodlands in the subtropical zone consist of trees spread widely apart, with grass and shrubs between them. There is not enough rain throughout the year for forests to grow. In Australia, many **eucalyptus** trees grow in the subtropical zone. The grasslands in subtropical areas are called tropical grasslands or savannas. Trees, grasses, and other plants that grow on savannas have special features to help them survive in dry periods. Some of these are:

- long roots that reach down to underground water
- trunks that can store water
- leaves that drop off in the dry season to help save water
- underground storage **bulbs**

Animals

Most animals on savannas have long legs to help them travel long distances to search for food and water. Others are able to burrow underground, where it is cooler. There are many **grazing** animals on savannas because there is a lot of room to move around and a lot of grass to eat.

A gazelle herd in the Serengeti, northern Tanzania.

Arid Zone

The arid zone has a very dry climate. Areas that have an arid climate turn into desert. The ground in a desert is covered with dry soil, sand, pebbles, and rock, and there are few plants. There is little rainfall.

Hot Deserts

Most deserts are hot deserts, where it is very hot during the day. The skies have no clouds because there is little moisture in the air. Deserts get very cold at night because there is no cloud cover to stop the warmth from escaping.

Weather Report

In hot deserts there may be no rain for years, but then it can rain heavily, bringing floods.

Monument Valley in Utah is located in the arid zone.

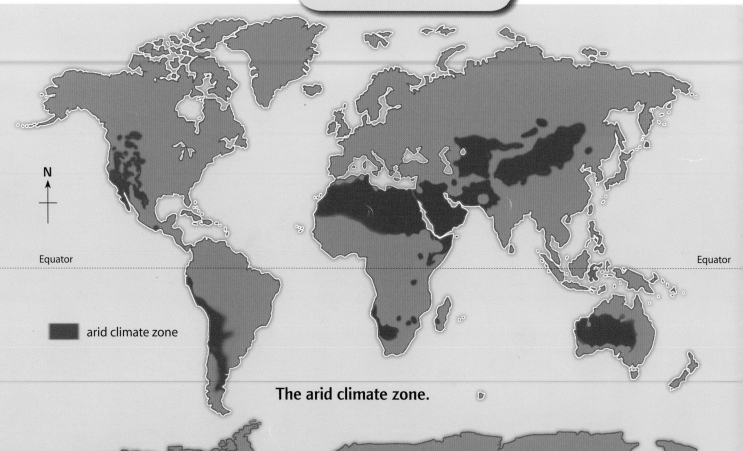

N

Equator

Equator

arid climate zone

The arid climate zone.

Cold Deserts

Some deserts are cold. These deserts, such as the Gobi Desert in Asia, have snow in winter and never get warm enough for many plants to grow.

Vegetation

Some parts of hot deserts have no plants at all, but most areas have some low-growing shrubs and short trees. These plants survive the hot, dry conditions by storing water or having hard, spiny leaves that prevent water loss. After rain, a hot desert can become green as small plants **germinate** and flower. These plants soon die, but they leave their seeds behind for the next time it rains.

Most cold deserts have only grass and moss that grow in the spring. Some areas have low shrubs scattered about.

Animals

The animals in desert areas are mainly animals that dig burrows. They burrow underground in hot deserts to escape the heat, and in cold deserts to keep warm. Some deserts have grazing animals that move around looking for food and water. Antelopes can live in cold and hot deserts, and camels live in hot deserts.

For a few short weeks after rain, this hot desert is covered with green plants and their flowers.

The Australian quokka lives in an arid environment.

Semiarid Zone

Places in the semiarid zone are dry, but not as dry as deserts. These climates have grassland areas with low rainfall. The grasslands have different names around the world. They are called:

- *prairie* in North America
- *pampas* in South America
- *steppe* in Russia
- the *outback* or grasslands in Australia
- *veldt* or semiarid savanna in Africa

Places with a semiarid climate can have long **droughts**. When this happens, the land becomes very dry. Wildfires kill off the old grass, which allows new grass to grow.

Precipitation

There is enough **precipitation** in semiarid areas to allow grass and some other plants to grow, such as a few trees. There is not enough rain for forests to grow.

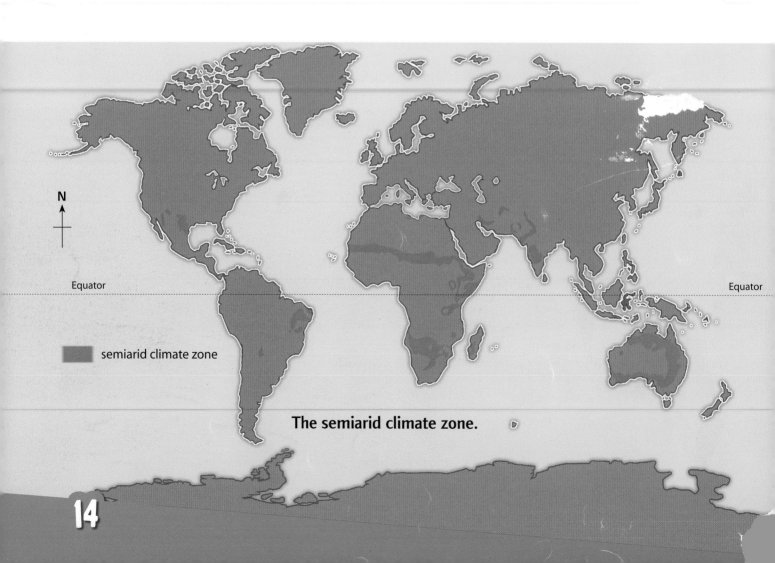

Equator

Equator

N

semiarid climate zone

The semiarid climate zone.

Vegetation

Grasses in the semiarid zone have narrow, waxy leaves to keep moisture in. They have long roots to get water from deep in the soil and also to store water. These roots help the grass to recover from fire and from being eaten by grazing animals.

Animals

As in the subtropical climate, animals have long legs to help them move quickly over the wide-open spaces. Both of these climate zones are home to herds of large grazing animals, which eat grass most of the time.

Animals and Birds in a Semiarid Climate

Continent	Types of Animals and Birds
Africa	zebras, giraffes, ostriches, and wildebeest
North America	buffalo, bald eagles, wolves, coyotes, and prairie dogs
South America	rhea, pampas cats, and pampas foxes
Europe/Asia	horses, antelopes, wolves, and falcons
Australia	kangaroos, emus, rabbits, and eagles

Wildebeest migrate across the Serengeti National Park in Tanzania every year to find good grazing land.

Mediterranean Zone

The Mediterranean zone has hot, dry summers and cool, wet winters. The hot weather can last for up to five months, and be extremely dry. This climate is found in the area around the Mediterranean Sea, which is where it gets its name. The Mediterranean climate is also found in other places around the world, such as southern California, Cape Town, South Africa, and southwestern Australia.

Vegetation

Land in the Mediterranean zone often has flat plains, rocky hills, or mountain slopes. These areas are covered with scrub, woodland, or eucalypt forests. Droughts are common in this climate zone. With the dry summers and the extra dryness brought by drought, wildfires can be common.

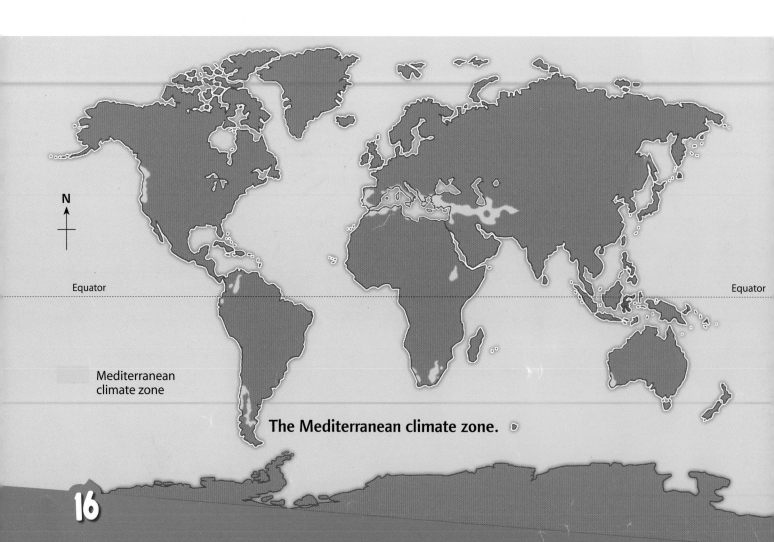

N

Equator

Equator

Mediterranean climate zone

The Mediterranean climate zone.

The rocky hills of Sicily, Italy, are typical of the Mediterranean zone.

Wildfires

Wildfires help some of the plants living in this climate to grow. Their seed coats and seed pods are opened by the heat of the fire.

Plants in the Mediterranean climate can survive the very hot, dry summers and the wildfires they bring. Most of them have small, hard leaves that hold moisture. Cacti and other plants that store water live in these areas.

Animals

Desert and grassland animals live in the Mediterranean zone because they can handle the hot, dry summers. Some can burrow underground, some have tough feet, and some have long legs for moving across large distances. These animals include coyotes, jack rabbits, mule deer, wolves, jackals, foxes, mountain lions, skunks, and wild goats.

Temperate Zone

The temperate zone has four distinct seasons: summer, fall, winter, and spring. There is a big difference between the summer and winter temperatures, and temperatures often change from day to day. In temperate climates there is usually good rainfall all year, generally with more rain in summer.

Features of the Four Seasons

In the spring, the weather becomes warmer and rainfall is good. **Deciduous** plants flower and grow new leaves.

Summers are warm or hot, with good rainfall.

In all temperate climates except Australia, there are forests of deciduous trees. In the fall, the leaves on deciduous trees change color. By the end of the fall, the leaves have dropped off the trees, and the branches remain bare during the winter.

Winter in a temperate climate is colder in areas that are farther away from the coast. On the coast, the temperature is usually above 32 degrees Fahrenheit (0 degrees Celsius). Inland, it can be so cold that there is snow and ice.

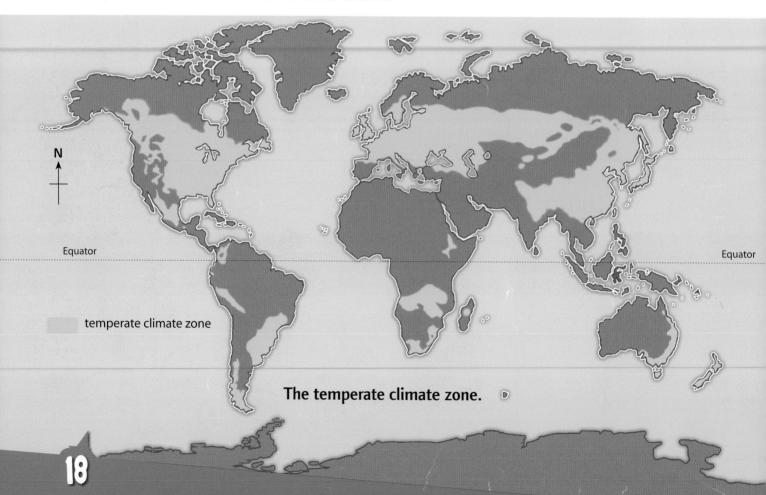

N

Equator

Equator

temperate climate zone

The temperate climate zone.

Vegetation

Temperate forests have very tall trees, such as oak, beech, elm, and gum trees. Lower down there are plants such as rhododendrons, azaleas, mountain laurel and tree ferns, and young trees. Ferns, herbs, lichen, and mosses grow closer to the ground.

Animals

Animals that live in the temperate zone have to cope with warm summers and cold winters, and with a change in their food supply from season to season. Some animals **hibernate** in the winter and live off the land in the other three seasons.

Trees provide shelter for animals. They get food and water from them.

Red pandas live in Asian temperate forests and are a protected species.

Animals and Birds in a Temperate Climate

Location	Types of Animals and Birds
North America	bears, beavers, foxes, deer, mountain lions, rabbits, and woodpeckers
Europe/Asia	boars, badgers, squirrels, and red pandas
Australia	koalas, opossums, wallabies, wombats, and kookaburras
New Zealand	kiwis, kea, and morepork

Northern Temperate Zone

The northern temperate climate has short, cool summers and long, very cold winters. There is fairly heavy rain in the short summer season and heavy snow in the winter. The overall rainfall is not very high. This type of climate is only found on continents in the northern **hemisphere**.

In this climate, the soils become waterlogged when the land thaws in the spring. They often stay soggy because there is a layer of permanently frozen soil underneath.

Conifers have waxy, needlelike leaves. This wax gives protection from the freezing temperatures.

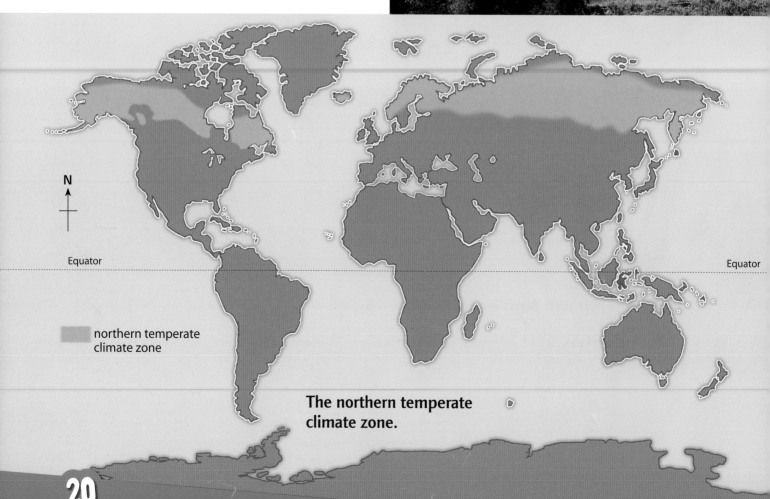

N

Equator

Equator

northern temperate climate zone

The northern temperate climate zone.

Vegetation

There are not many kinds of plants that can survive the winter in the northern temperate zone. The trees in boreal forests are mostly conifers such as spruces, pines, and firs. Conifers are trees that have needlelike leaves, and cones instead of flowers. There are some deciduous trees in boreal forests as well, such as maples, birches, and willows. Lichen and mosses grow on the ground.

Animals

Predatory animals in the boreal forests include the lynx, wolverine, mink, ermine, and sable. Their **prey** are animals such as hares, squirrels, and lemmings. There are also large plant-eaters such as elk and moose.

In the summer, there are millions of insects in the forests. Insect-eating birds fly north to these forests to breed in summer.

Weather Report

The northern temperate zone is known as the **Taiga**. The forests in the Taiga are called boreal forests—boreal means northern.

Elk feed on grass, leaves, and bark in the northern temperate zone.

Polar Zone

The polar zone is very cold. This zone is found around Earth's North and South Poles. Much of this land is covered with thick ice sheets and **glaciers**. The ice also spreads out over the ocean. There is snow on the ice sheets and the weather is dry and windy.

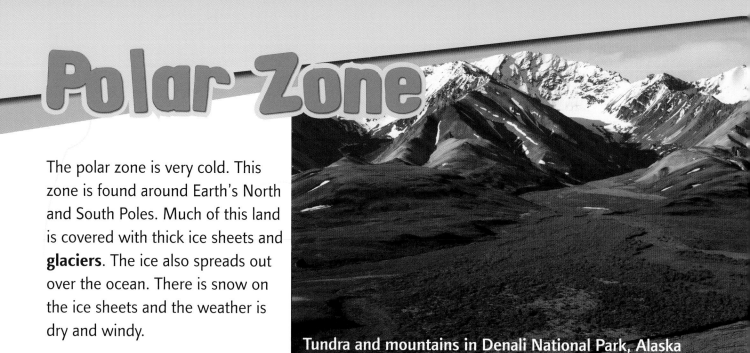

Tundra and mountains in Denali National Park, Alaska

Tundra

Tundra is the land in polar areas not covered by thick ice. It is a treeless area with strong, dry winds and low precipitation in the form of rain and snow. Much of the land in the **Arctic** is tundra. There is a small area of tundra in **Antarctica**.

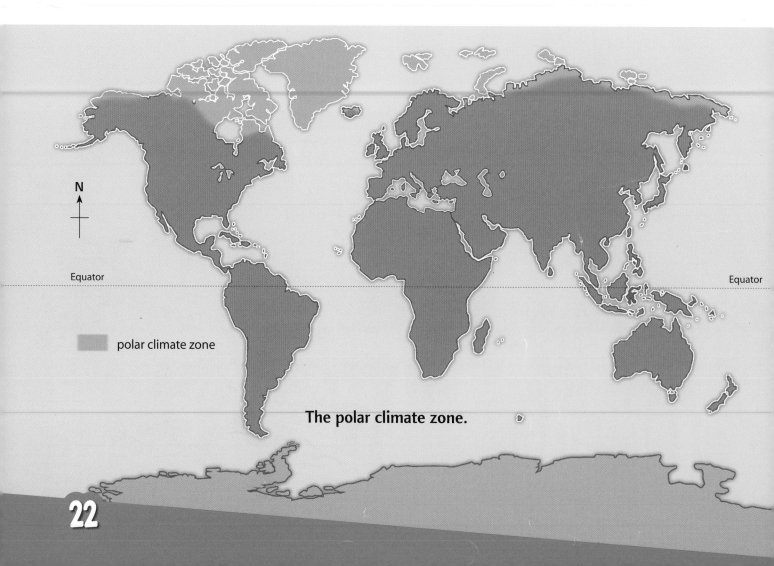

N

Equator   Equator

polar climate zone

The polar climate zone.

Vegetation

The tundra has a layer of permanently frozen soil below the surface called permafrost. Permafrost stops large plants from growing on the tundra. Low-growing plants such as mosses, lichens, and grasses are able to grow. Permafrost also stops water from sinking into the soil, which results in lakes and **marshes** forming.

Animals

Animals in the polar zone have many features to help them survive the harsh weather. They often have large bodies because this helps them to keep warm. They also have thick fur or feathers. Arctic foxes have coats that are light brown in the summer, to blend with tundra plants. Their coats turn white in the winter, to blend with snow. Many polar animals eat fish.

Weather Report

Polar areas have long, dark winters and short summers with weak sunlight.

Animals and Birds in the Polar Climate Zone

Area	Types of Animals and Birds
North Pole	caribou (reindeer), musk oxen, polar bears, seals, walruses, arctic foxes, arctic hares, and snowy owls
South Pole	seals and penguins

Polar bears have fur on their feet so that they don't slip on the ice.

Mountain Zone

The Andes Mountains make up the longest mountain range in the world.

The tops of high mountains have different climates from the valleys below. They are colder and have stronger winds and more snow. The air is also thinner, because the mountain peaks are so high. This means there is less **oxygen** for plants and animals. The mountain climate zone is also called the alpine climate.

The mountain climate is found in several places around the world, for example:

- the Rocky Mountains in North America
- the Andes in South America
- the Alps in Europe
- Mount Kilimanjaro in Africa
- the Himalayas in Tibet
- Mount Fuji in Japan

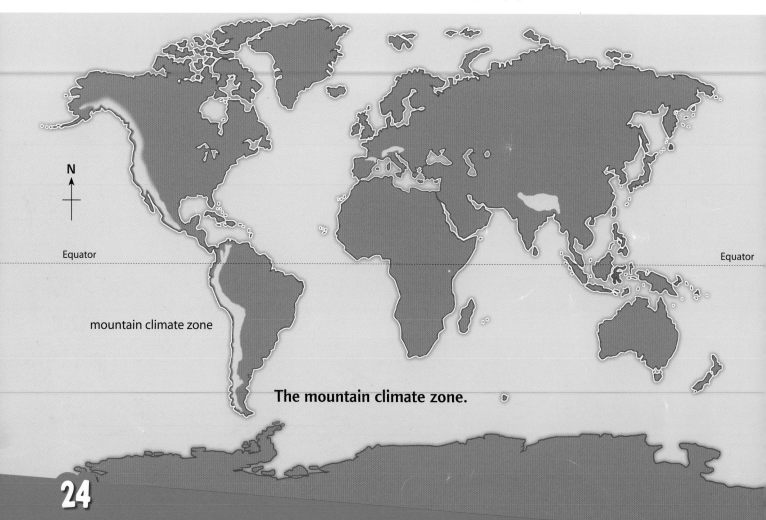

N

Equator

Equator

mountain climate zone

The mountain climate zone.

Vegetation

Plants such as tough, low-growing grasses and shrubs grow on high mountain slopes. They can live in the ice-cold, windy conditions.

Animals

Animals also have ways to cope with the cold, the rocky ground, and the thin air.

- The alpaca lives in the Andes Mountains in South America. It has very thick fur. Its long neck helps it to spot predators among the rocks of the mountain slopes.

- The snow leopard lives in the Himalayan alpine regions of central Asia. Its spotted coat allows it to blend in with the rocks. The thick fur on the soles of its feet keeps its paws warm in the snow. The inside of its nose is large to help it get enough oxygen.

Weather Report

The tops of the tallest mountains have snow on them all year round.

Mountain goats live in the Rocky Mountains of North America. They climb on steep, rocky mountainsides. They have double coats of white hair.

What Makes a Climate?

The climate of an area depends on many things, such as:

- the distance from the equator
- ocean currents
- the shape of the land
- winds

Distance from the Equator

Climates become warmer the closer they are to the equator. This is because the Sun is overhead or nearly overhead in these areas, so the Sun feels hotter. Farther from the equator, the Sun is lower in the sky, so it does not feel as hot.

Shape of the Land

Climates are affected by the shape of the land.

- Places that are inland have more extreme temperatures than places that are near coasts.
- Places that are near mountains are affected by the way mountains change winds.
- Places that are high above sea level have cooler climates with more clouds and precipitation.

Temperatures are less extreme near the sea than they are inland.

Ocean Currents

Water in Earth's oceans flows in rivers called ocean currents. Some ocean currents carry warm water and others carry cold water.

Warm Currents

Warm currents warm up the air above them. As it rises, the warm air picks up moisture from the sea and makes rain-filled clouds. If wind blows this air over land, it will probably cause rain there. Land near seas with warm currents often has good rainfall, such as eastern Australia.

Weather Report

A warm ocean current flows past the coast of northwestern Europe, which makes it warmer there than other places that are the same distance from the equator.

Cold Currents

Cold currents cool the air above them, which makes the air sink. This air will not develop clouds. If this air is blown over land it will not bring rain. Land near cold currents is often dry, such as the west coast of South America.

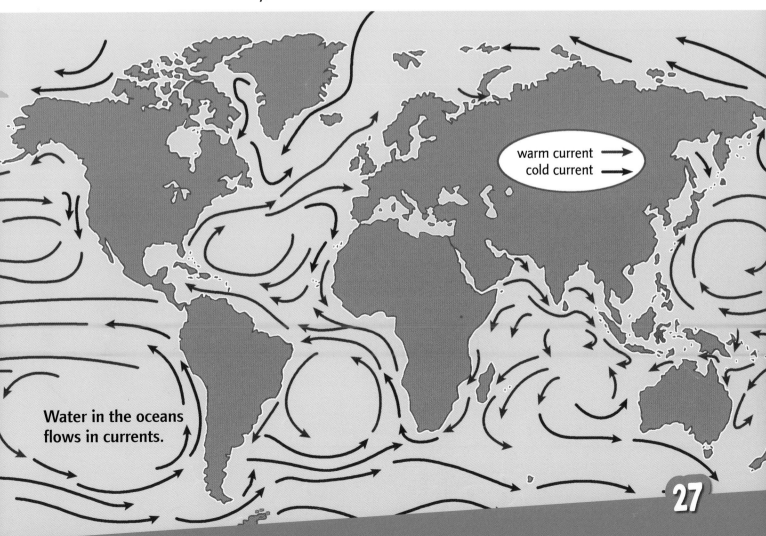

warm current ⟶
cold current ⟶

Water in the oceans flows in currents.

Winds

Winds affect the climate by carrying air that may be warm, cool, damp, or dry. Winds are usually named after the direction they come from, such as west wind or northeast wind.

Global Winds

Air in Earth's atmosphere circulates in a pattern. This creates winds at the surface that blow in the same direction year after year. These winds are known as trade winds, westerlies, and polar easterlies.

Prevailing Winds

The prevailing wind of an area is the wind that usually blows in that area. Often the prevailing wind is a global wind such as a trade wind. Local factors such as mountains bring local winds, which can cause the prevailing wind to blow from a different direction.

Weather Report

Chinook winds are warm winter winds that blow down the east side of the Rocky Mountains in North America. They have been known to melt deep snow very quickly.

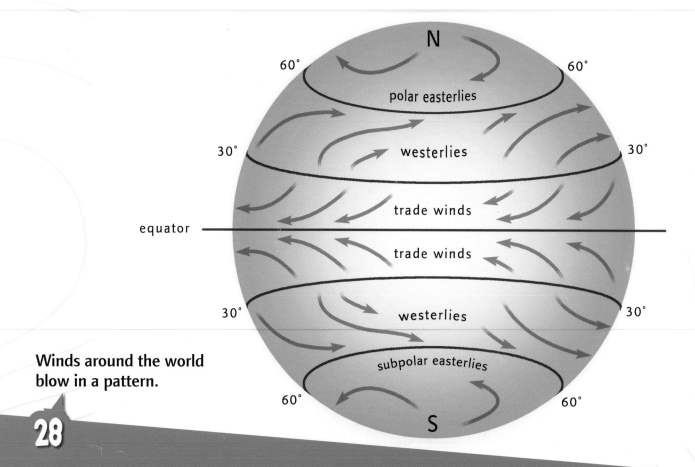

Winds around the world blow in a pattern.

Prevailing Winds and Climate

Together, prevailing winds and ocean currents influence an area's climate.

If the prevailing wind of an area blows from over the ocean, it warms the land if the ocean is warm, and cools the land if the ocean is cold. Also, warm air is moist, so wind that blows from over a warm sea will bring clouds and rain.

When the prevailing wind of an area has come from over hot land, the wind will be hot. If it blows from cold places, it will bring cold air. Both hot and cold air can bring rain if there is moisture in the area.

Cool breezes often blow in from the sea in the afternoons.

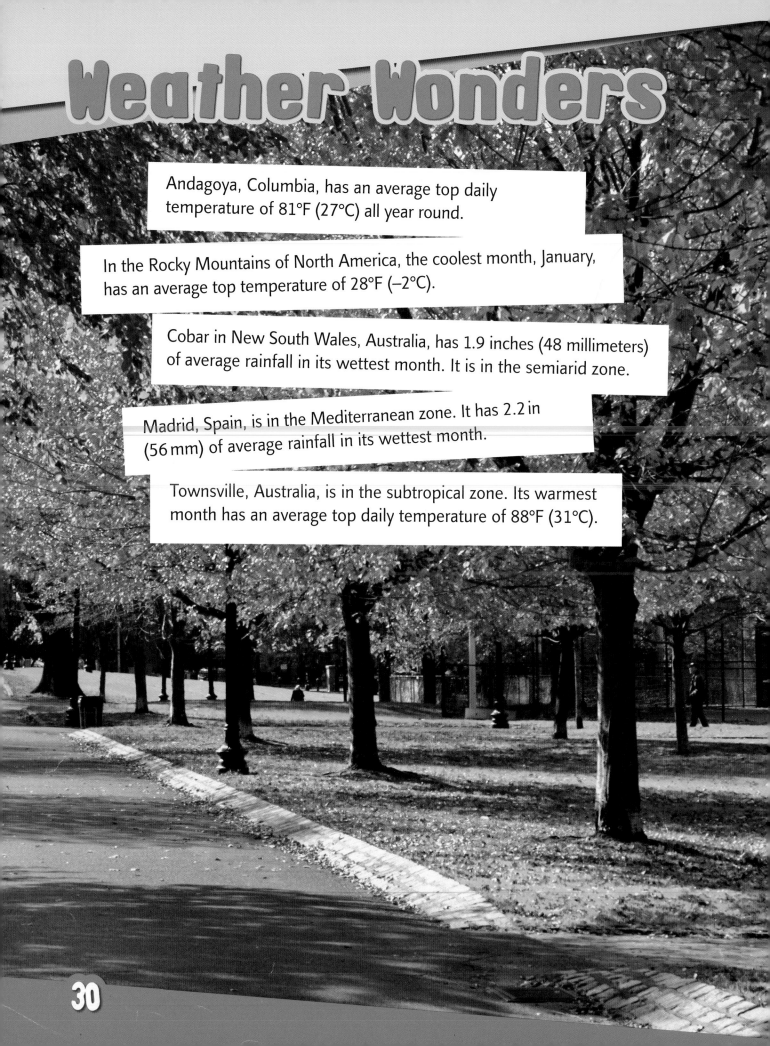

Weather Wonders

Andagoya, Columbia, has an average top daily temperature of 81°F (27°C) all year round.

In the Rocky Mountains of North America, the coolest month, January, has an average top temperature of 28°F (–2°C).

Cobar in New South Wales, Australia, has 1.9 inches (48 millimeters) of average rainfall in its wettest month. It is in the semiarid zone.

Madrid, Spain, is in the Mediterranean zone. It has 2.2 in (56 mm) of average rainfall in its wettest month.

Townsville, Australia, is in the subtropical zone. Its warmest month has an average top daily temperature of 88°F (31°C).

Glossary

Antarctica large continent at Earth's South Pole

Arctic area on and around Earth's North Pole

bulbs thickened or round underground parts of plants that store food

cumulus has a puffy, rounded shape

deciduous trees that lose their leaves in the fall

deserts very dry areas that receive very little rainfall

droughts periods of less rain than normal for months or years

equator imaginary line around the middle of Earth that is the boundary between the northern and southern hemispheres

eucalyptus type of evergreen tree, such as a gum tree

forests places where many trees grow close together

germinate begin to grow from a seed

glaciers large rivers of slow-moving ice, made from hardened snow

grazing eating grass and leaves

hemisphere half a sphere; for example, either the top (north) or bottom (south) half of Earth

hibernate sleep through winter

humid a high level of moisture in the air

marshes areas of low, wet land

oxygen gas animals and plants breathe and take in, in order to live

poles top and bottom of Earth

precipitation rain, snow, or hail that falls to the ground

predatory animals that hunt and eat other animals

prey animals eaten by other animals

rain forests forests that grow in warm areas with very high rainfall

temperatures measures of how much heat is in something

vegetation type of plants that grow in an area

woodlands lands covered by trees and vegetation

Index